Kitty Donnelly

In Dangerous Hours

Indigo Dreams Publishing

First Edition: In Dangerous Hours
First published in Great Britain in 2022 by:
Indigo Dreams Publishing
24, Forest Houses
Cookworthy Moor
Halwill
Beaworthy
Devon
EX21 5UU

www.indigodreamspublishing.com

Kitty Donnelly has asserted her right under the Copyright, Designs and Patents Act 1988 to be identified as the author of this work.
© Kitty Donnelly 2022

ISBN 978-1-912876-69-3

British Library Cataloguing in Publication Data. A CIP record for this book can be obtained from the British Library.

This book is sold subject to the condition that it shall not, by way of trade or otherwise, be lent, re-sold, hired out, or otherwise circulated without the author's and publisher's prior consent in any form of binding or cover other than that in which it is published and without a similar condition including this condition being imposed on the subsequent purchaser.

Designed and typeset in Palatino Linotype by Indigo Dreams.
Cover design by Ronnie Goodyer at Indigo Dreams
Printed and bound in Great Britain by 4edge Ltd.

Papers used by Indigo Dreams are recyclable products made from wood grown in sustainable forests following the guidance of the Forest Stewardship Council.

For my mum, Susan & my sister, Sarah

Acknowledgements

Thank you to the following magazines, journals, anthologies & podcasts for publishing/broadcasting versions of these poems: Acumen; Abridged; Boats Against the Current; *Dear Dylan* (Indigo Dreams); Dreich; Eat the Storms; Fevers of the Mind; Galway Review; The Honest Ulsterman; Ink Sweat and Tears; Interim; Manchester Writing School 'Write Where We Are Now' pandemic poetry project; Mslexia; Nine Pens *Hair Raising Anthology*; Poetry Birmingham Literary Journal; Poems from the Heron Clan; The Pandemic Poetry Anthology; *Poetic Map of Freedom* (Southwark Council); Stepaway Magazine; The Rialto; *Wild Nature Poetry Award* (Indigo Dreams); 192 Magazine.

Some of these poems have been inspired by the following inspirational women, fictional characters & novels. Emily Bronte (1818-1848). Vivienne Eliot (1888-1947). Zelda Sayre Fitzgerald (1900-1948). *Rebecca* by Daphne du Maurier. 'Fifth Helena Drive' is the last address of Marilyn Monroe (1926-1962). Jean Rhys (1890-1979). Characters 'Laura Palmer' & 'Leyland Palmer' are from the TV series *Twin Peaks* created by David Lynch & Mark Frost. 'Weeping Woman Seated on a Basket' is based on the Vincent Van Gough painting of the same title. 'Tree Shadows on the Park Wall' is based on the John Atkinson Grimshaw painting. Bridget O'Donnell from County Clare appeared in the *Illustrated London News* in 1849. The sketch of her and her starving children became a symbol of the suffering inflicted by the Great Irish Famine. 'The Legend of the Long Woman' was inspired by the novel *The Long Woman's Grave* by Hugo Donnelly (1951-2003). 'Jennifer Fairgate' was the pseudonym of an unknown woman who checked into the Plaza Hotel in Oslo in 1995 & was found dead in her room, presumably by suicide. Her real identity has never been established.

Thank you to Ronnie Goodyer & Dawn Bauling at Indigo Dreams. Your continued belief in me has helped me to continue writing & your warmth & passion is valued more than I can say. I am lucky to have had the support of Anna Saunders, including her inspiring workshops, brilliant verse & her championing of my poetry.

Thanks to the Jerwood Compton Fellowship for their support, & to Colin Bancroft, Creative Futures, Damien B Donnelly, Melissa Lee-Houghton for her stunning artwork & generous words, Nigel Kent, Josephine Lay & Crafty Crows, Manchester Writing School, Jenny Mitchell for the prompt that inspired 'Freedom's' & to Natalie Scott.

Thanks to M, who I couldn't love more, & to Pat Donnelly for his detailed research into our Irish family tree.

'Love in a Pandemic' & 'Exchanging Presents' are for M.
'Tearing Poppies' is for Evie.
'The Comb' & 'Coda' are for Hugo Donnelly.

CONTENTS

Kingfisher	11
Clemency	12
Light	13
Three Deer Descending	14
The Goldfinch	15
Emily Bronte: 1846	16
Monsters & Angels	17
Twin Peaks: Falling	18
High	19
Wreckers	20
Interrupted	21
Zelda Fitzgerald: Synaesthesia	22
Legend of the Long Woman	23
The Crisis Team	24
Derelict	25
The Comb	26
Tree Shadows on the Park Wall	27
Sour Cherry	28
Laura Palmer: Waiting for Leland	29
Invasions	30
Out of Body	31
Fifth Helena Drive	32
Fairy Tale	33
Twin Peaks: One Eyed Jacks	34
Vows	35
Exchanging Presents	36
Weeping Woman Seated on a Basket	37
'Jennifer Fairgate'	38
Prey	39
Jean Rhys: Lost Letter	40
Love in a Pandemic	41
Zelda Fitzgerald: Dear Scott	42
Freedom's	43
Rebecca de Winter: In the Dangerous Hours	44

Loss Of An Animal	45
Bridget O'Donnell: Hunger	46
Tearing Poppies	47
Vivienne Eliot: Dear Tom	48
Seven Year Itch	49
Dartmoor Ponies	50
Anosmia	51
Storm Francis	52
Second Time Around	53
Night Terrors	54
1 Paradise Street	55
Where Your Voice Is	57
Test Results	58
Rebecca de Winter: After Diagnosis	59
Laura Palmer: Diary Redacted	60
Surfacing	61
Shrine	62
Dewsbury Country Park	63
Barn Sparrows of Chernobyl	64
Prank Caller	65
Prayer	67
Coda	68
Limerick	69
Call Sixteen	70
Female Tawny Waiting	71
Playing Dead	72

In Dangerous Hours

"It was the hour between dog and wolf, as they say…"

~ Jean Rhys, *After Leaving Mr MacKenzie*

Kingfisher

It was a sign: pure lapis on the post
plunged into canal sediment.

It surveyed its territory, paused & darted
under Lock 9, a featherweight

jewel flicked on the wind.
Returning fishless, its head revolved

towards the glass where I stood,
museum-frigid: my first live Kingfisher.

I should have tailed its poem
through the frosted dawn's distemper.

It was tempting me to follow it by pen,
to know it vivid & separate

from ossified kin: that feathered
gift of indurated velvet

with scratched black beads for eyes,
whose twiggy box I switched

for football cards,
unable to stand the cloy of mold,

too old to poke my finger in the rag-hole.
Now it had risen: fallen constellations

etched across each wing,
urging me to drown my laptop,

ditch my boots, flit with it
through the waterlogged morning.

Clemency

Weeks, strong sun has seared the soil,
incongruent, luring us out
as though it were natural
for summer to crown in April.
The valley swelters, febrile
under lockdown: hearts leaping
at each new symptom,
temperatures checked like the time.

I want lightening cracking over the heath,
thunder clapping like Thursdays' hands,
a high wind, loosed like relief.
Who took for granted the gift
of effortless breaths; reassurance
an arm through an arm can give;
lips on lips, hair brushing a cheek?
I did, I did.

Light

before the day decides   light
Sunday light   hungry   light
the colour of absence   insistent   light
light that pries the curtains like a crowbar
light   dark gold but miserly with meaning
light that sticks like a lump in the throat
stagnant   light   shall-I-shall-I-not   light
light caught in the water jug
light   violent with hope
why do you hate this word   light?
I will force feed you   light
by tongue   by poem
light have you not spent up all your   darkness?
in hours strung with diaphanous purpose
remember bleakest moments are   pre-   light

Three Deer Descending

We swerve into the darkest quarter of a year
so black we barely see the turning coming.
No bonfires, gatherings, communal toasts.
Even ghosts are isolating.

As the sun mulls over the valley, I turn the bend
onto Grimescar Road & Huddersfield,
a Grimshaw landscape.
I'm driving centuries to work.

On the tightest curve,
three roe deer descend in sequence.
I sweep past to a clinic filthy with distress.
I'll sit head in hands between patients,

those deer hoofing down the slope forgotten.
Nursing, nursing with heart, pickpockets the poem.

The Goldfinch

It died quietly on my palm,
externally unruffled,
its body just beyond
a living warmth. I fought the dual
tragedy & privilege of holding it,
unsure at first which bird it was
on the turn of becoming.
A jag of lemon lightening
across each wing, red-masked,
I recalled the Fabritius painting:
wall-fixed perch, chain clasped
like an iron rosary to a claw-foot
sore from the wings'
insistent rising, the expression
marked by an uptilt of the chin
like a child supressing, with pride,
their furious griefs.

Emily Bronte: 1846

Today I asked *Papa, please let me have*
the lightening patterned cloth.
He said, *Emily, yes,*
though I owe him one pound five shillings.
After, I walked breezily to Ponden Kirk.

My boots are drying on the hearth.
Charlotte is pestering
I very much need to hear your writings.
I lock my papers in the desk-box.
Tomorrow I'll be Heathcliff

tidying the peat house.
Anne will play Cathy peeling turnips,
though she doesn't know.
This book enchants me so,
like moonlight on gravestones.

Monsters & Angels

All was comparison: waistlines, lifelines, star signs,
Sharpie tattoos. We counted moles & freckles,
painted fingernails with Tipex. Menstruation began
like a private assault by ourselves on ourselves.
Some stuffed wads of tissues into knickers, too ashamed
to confess to their mothers another expense.

You shaved your legs with a market pinched Gillette.
Most of us, in lukewarm baths, scraped fibulas
with rusty Bics. Lads aimed their footballs at our heads,
projected lust by gobbing in our schoolbags.
We scrawled obscenities on plywood boards
that hid the fractured glass your mother's boyfriend fisted.

We smelled of Dewberry, White Musk, Vanilla Fields.
Your permed hair splayed, each corkscrew stiff with Elnett.

Twin Peaks: Falling

We were lying on the couch when you first told
about the men, the casino, the lodge.

Perhaps not *exactly* a casino, a lodge,
more The Railway Inn & council flats,

but men, certainly: their hands, how
many decades they were older than us.

When he pulled me in for a kiss (his reward
for finding my jade ring) there was disgust,

then deeper layers of disgust disguised
as indifference. Who wants a tongue in their mouth?

Me, you said & your pupils dilated.
I knew you were falling through space.

High

An arctic tern will fly 10,000 miles
to flourish in two summers worth of light;

so I was high after he died, chasing
sun on the wing, though directionless.

I swallowed three green capsules every night,
peristalsis pulsing them

through my scorched oesophagus.
I took what I could get

to alter consciousness,
testing my fragmented sense of time

against the wall clock's competence
till dawn was salmon red

& gutted on the banks of the horizon.
I was not or even near myself.

Wreckers

You type of Cheltenham summers
scorched like spoons;

how you detest needles, their poisons
choking mainlines first, then calves, thighs, toes.

When those veins are sunken threads,
you probe your groin for inroads.

I swallow a scatter of pills on my palm
three hundred miles north.

No foil, no pipes, no gauze
but farms where cockerels vaunt each dawn

with clownish gusto. Boats off Sellafield
net phosphorescent mackerel.

I wear my mother's half-mast pants,
tagged *Edinburgh Woollen Mill.*

We walk close to the edge of the cliffs,
you and I, fellow wreckers luring our own ships,

lighters flickering from coves like flinty lanterns.

Interrupted

Numb, playing the role of someone else,
I swapped grief for grapplings,
crushed thighs, hair pinned beneath elbows,

not grasping how intimacy's brute,
pummelling connections
are invasions if the mind's not also touched.

Personality's a movable feast,
a product of circumstance in constant flux.
Months I was that woman I admired least;

months I didn't write or read.
Libraries of afternoons I sat while children
thrashed in ball pool seas

of arid blues & greens, barbeque fat
greasing my hair & *Okay* splayed
across my sticky knees.

Zelda Fitzgerald: Synaesthesia

Flowers bloomed too vividly that spring.
Each word pulsed like a swollen tongue.
Faces shrank to distance.

Heads cranked back on necks too thin
& the Seine was cerulean blue,
bleeding its canvas.

We stopped speaking.
I craved the anchor of your voice,
even scolding or blind drunk

on disenchantment.
I didn't tell you when the streets began
to smell of ants, or how the city

liquified at night, a molten silk.
You drank. I practised, practised
fainting on a diet of pirouettes.

Then all my hard-won courage sagged.
I smashed the stage-set of our lives:
tore gowns, burnt paintings,

cast off my necklace of stars
& flew through Montparnasse,
feral in ballet shoes.

Legend of the Long Woman

In the lug of the rocks   *look*
look at your life with eyes
that captive viewed the world
too long through slits.

Bogland dilates Lorcan's pupils
its expanse a sunken heaven
of possibilities
achieved   by endurance.

Cauthleen stoops over a tarn
where light is unlicensed
    bleak as heath   her reflection
non-existent   she hears wind

knotting reeds   uncombing hair
smells loss like autumn
rot   an ending
tastes landscapes

of sorrows   their flavour   hunger.
Disappointment thickens
her blood   clots hope   she topples
slowly   a tower

shivering in space until gravity
snatches it   body meets turf.
Carlingford Lough   quivers.
An eighth wave overcomes the tide.

In Omeath   candles snuff themselves.
She's buried   buried where she falls
& long   she lies long in the peat
of her thwarted heart.

The Crisis Team

tonight is just three women
in an ancient cotton mill hunched over desks.
No doctor to prescribe, no psychiatric beds.
We're spread thin as labelled milk
in the shared kitchen, the locked-away cake.

I make a foul fruit tea.
Through a window on the Bradford Rd,
a kebab spins slowly on a spit.
The world feels grey & gristly.
Shrunken, reconstituted.

There is little care & more demand for it.
Patients – in the void between need & provision –
are shouting, while nurses curl & stiffen,
        falling one by one –

Derelict

If I love you it's 'cos I'm drawn to
hollow buildings   shattered glass
fissured sinks sobbing rusty tears,
because I need to know *who goes there?* –
There's an echo in your eyes,
you're sadder than a sparrow on a seedless feeder,

bleak as a locked playground, the puddled
roundabout seized on its axis. You bring to mind
dank railway bridges lit by a canal-reflected
moon   freight trains trundling overhead.
You're all these things, both
wrecked & resurrected.

If I love you it's because you're empty,
                        brimming with emptiness.

The Comb

You were always disappointed
that you couldn't have a Beatles fringe:
glossy, straight, Top of the Pops slick.
Your hair grew upwards, black, thick,
coarse Northern Irish.

You had one comb I knew of
my whole life & kept it always in your
left jacket pocket. Now I have it.
It made no difference anyway.
I never saw you use it.

When you knew you were ill,
before diagnosis, you hacked
your hair to half an inch.
Questioned by colleagues, you claimed
you'd been cast as Magwitch

in a Minehead production of Great Expectations,
which meant *fuck off*, which meant
it's none of your fucking business.
The chemo was called 5-Fluorouracil.
Even with a sherry & a smoke at night,

nausea crippled you: *worse than pain*.
Still your hair grew, thinner,
but no great cascade on the pillow.
You were glad of it for the first time,
its magnitude, its drug-defying perseverance.

In the chapel of rest, I touched it –
your hair – the only thing I dared to,
not easy with refrigerated skin, & alabaster
angels clasping hands above the coffin.
I coiled my Ulster curl into your palm.

Tree Shadows on the Park Wall

There's a woman on the path.
We see only her back, cloaked & hooded
already on the brink of distance,
as though we watchers missed
her twilit face through tardiness.
To her right's a wall with shadows
caught in moon-cast branches.
She's not in the clear yet.

Trees mesh, arcing the dirt road;
cart tracks scribble peripheries
of Roundhay Park. Will she pass
through the gate? Is that swerve
in the lane to a safer place? Who's waiting?
I'm afraid for her in this off-milk light.

Sour Cherry

We knew there was something amiss
when the cherry spat its unripe marbles.
Though boughs looked lime-green fresh,
each leaf was pocked with buck-shot holes,
crisped around the edges.

We drank homebrew on the bench,
flicking through diseases,
discovering fungus,
sporing since autumn,
was spreading in the April budding.

Then your feet were on the top rung,
the scrape of the bowsaw severing branches
with centres like lead pencils or furred arteries.
We rewintered it, hoping
to resurrect it with our amputations.

Only at bedtime, when beer
was repossessed by the liver, & the tree
stood stiff in the shear of its new shadow,
did we realise its leaves were a loss
on the curtain: an inverse, absent pattern.

Laura Palmer: Waiting for Leland

Have you known Bob, mother?
We cook supper in the season of rotten onions.
Our talk is false. Beneath falsity
a yearning for connection.
The ceiling fan whirrs
Dad will be home; Dad will be home soon.
Mother did you go into the woods against your will?
She passes the steak knife,
takes a pill with Chardonnay.

At first it was a rush: the coke,
the cheap lights pulsing on & off in neon.
BANG! BANG! COME! DON'T COME.
I was flush with that special dirty desire
that expires to seediness.
Mother, do you ever venture so far
from who you were you crack the mirror
of your own reflection?
Power cuts & the steak stalls, red.

She stubs a cigarette on the draining board.
'Darn', she says. 'Darn, your father's back
& we've nothing but salad & bloody meat.'

Invasions

Those nests you point to
high in the birch by the railway line

are haustoria: mistletoe
siphoning silver,

darkening bark,
draining the crown.

I dreamt I was a limp wasp
chewing chambers of a bud

my mother's larvae
modified to gall.

I can't pinpoint
when our symbiosis shifted,

I became burl wood:
my abnormality shielding your parasite.

Out of Body

In a rented room, a tangle of limbs

                                        capture absence –

fractured images,

                                        a fault-line

between flesh and brain –

                                        a couple stumble in,

actors

                                        late for a film

already in progress:

                                        a man, a woman

conjoined, their bodies contorting

                                        in sticky darkness,

the soundtrack

                                        his quick breathing

hers –

Fifth Helena Drive

The shapes of things I've lost
define me, their outlines
precise absences   missing pieces
shadow shards.

I try rational approaches:
therapy   dissociation
barbiturate enemas –
nothing works.

A living thing's unique, once only.
Sobriety slides towards intoxication.
I undress quietly,
                    blackening my lashes.

Fairy Tale

Sick mornings, she hauled herself back to the bedsit.
She forgot her love of books: her shelves stark, her journal
blank pages. There was a woman with kohl-rimmed eyes
who consoled her: sometimes she stroked

her leg up to the thigh. She was the mother
of the boarding house, a confidant who turned
the hideous mundane. There was a prince (there always is) who
sweated in nightclubs, his whispers spitty with secrets.

He promised things. All was a sticky exchange,
a tower of power. The man at the summit –
'the king' he called himself –
had the soleless gaze of a deep sea fish.

Now middle aged, she wears her history on her face,
her mind snagged where her girlhood was corrupted.
Her 36 page letter to the Met's had no response as yet,
though it's been seven years.

The 'king' is dead. The prince has his wealth, his wife,
a shoebox of obscene images. That so-called mother
with the blackened lids? She runs a brothel in a novel
by John Irving in New Hampshire.

Twin Peaks: One Eyed Jacks

It's always just over the border, danger:
across county lines, a slide into territory
foreign & exciting. How soon do you realise

you're floundering? Is it when you decline
a drink & he thrusts you a treble shot,
chinking glass on glass, mouthing *down it?*

Is it a hand stuck up your dress on the way to the toilet?
You stare into a face, blank & mimicking – *so what*?
Is it when the woman snaps *hey kid in the school skirt,*

freshen my make-up, eyes widened to be rimmed
in black, hands all jitters from white lines?
Don't miss a bit & I'll give you one of these to wake you up –

Or when he yanks your arm & you whisper *I'm only fifteen*,
the scream's ascension tightening your throat?

Vows

Will you hold me with my scant illusions still aflame,
haul me from the crest of a violent dream,
steer me towards morning
when you'll drench the room in sun & find
the pillow cross-hatched on my cheek,
my dress slept-in?

Sometimes my tongue can run and run.
Sometimes I stumble into silence,
speech occluded. What of evenings
when our tempers bark like dogs,
the tread of patience bald & shallow –
will you stray from me then?

There are ghosts that go where I go.
Will you take with my hand theirs?

Exchanging Presents

For his birthday he wants an owl's hoot,
the flash of a fox, russet in russet
undergrowth. A tricky gift to give.
She desires an oak apple necklace:
holes for string already gall-wasp
burrowed through one side of each
borrowed bud; no jewellery, no Audi,
no exotic cruise but the warmth of fur
against her cheek; the shrew her cat
brought gently by mouth across
park & road to place, intact, at her feet.
He asks for candlelight where flames
weave stories; her arm around his back,
pressing with the safety of substantiality;
to sketch her when she flicks black wings
of eyeliner, wishing he *were* her.
She needs his morning racket guaranteed:
dishes clanging as he whistles with the robin.
If not these things   then nothing.

Weeping Woman Seated on a Basket

She crumples in the middle of her working day,
loss balled in her fists, tears slipping over wrists,
snaking down sleeves. How to carry this defeat?
How to complete chores with it,
heavy as an infant on her bony shoulders?
These are the captured coals of her grief.
Their flames elude the artist with their heat,
their raw humanity.

Though we weep in separate centuries,
it's to the same dark mirror.
Tell me she survived, rising from her basket,
striding out into a street that soiled
her skirt-hems, slipping into arms
that had the strength to hold her weight.

'Jennifer Fairgate'

Do Not Disturb dangled from the handle
when maids rattled past
with tea bags, laundered towels, toilet roll.

They assumed she was sleeping.

Within the hour, the hotel was crawling,
yellow tape partitioned the whole 8th floor.
A detective clumsily shrouded the body.

Luminol flared blue for blood.

Blackout blinds made a cave of the suite
they swore was double locked
from the inside, the TV on but muted.

The guest in 2805 did not exist.

Her given address was an address
once – demolished in 1976.
CCTV, of course, was out of service.

Smells of rotten fruit fused with *Eternity*.

She lay high in the sky above a city
where commuters clashed umbrellas.
In a small, splayed suitcase was her life:

all clothing labels carefully excised.

Prey

On the scratch mat, a perfectly excised mouse's heart
is laid out pink as a fingernail.
I've been here a while: can distinguish the fat
string of a rat's bowel; tell a shrew, long as wide,
from a black-eyed, beaver-faced vole.

I walk the gash between rain & rain
in animal tracks: the four-toed fox;
roe prints brimming with the Hebble's spill.
The terrier – mad on the scent of a split goose –
trails feathers to the forest's entrance.

Here voices trouble the brush;
a whisp of burning rises.
I'm conscious of bare skin below my knees,
of nothing in my fist but keys & above   only kites –
those gliding, tranquil witnesses.

Jean Rhys: Lost Letter

Now it's Beckenham.
Each time I make a dash for Paris
I end up back in the cul-de-sac,
a spring, retracting.

This system makes small lawmakers
of everyone: eager to report,
eager to be on the winning team.
I creep about in my own home.

As placid as I've been all year –
believe it or not! – the one night
when my temper flares,
that broken glass of wine…

They're on me like a pack of dogs,
drooling at the blue lights flashing.
They nose through my bins:
She calls herself a writer! Look at these bottles…

I call that something else…
That's the wit of the English for you, their sniggers.
How they cheer on your demise!
In a town of flapping Union Jacks

they play *I spy a stranger…*
I sit & wonder what hell may be full of.
Dear, we've got to laugh!
I dreamt it was gated by doctor's receptionists.

Love in a Pandemic

The house holds a charge:
static, percussive nausea.
I watch hot water
pummelling your hands,
split skin wing-thin.

Feeling the headache tick
behind my eyes, I take
your respiration rate.
Gathering inhalers for the night –
brown, blue, pink –

I catch a Tawny's
sanitary hoot,
realising this carless dark's
perfumed like childhood.

Zelda Fitzgerald: Dear Scott

I gave our marriage all I had, which was myself.
You recorded my aphorisms, syllable by syllable.

I found your female characters soluble,
remote, with princess tendencies,
want of hardship gifting their expressions
the privilege you mistook for beauty.

Who owns my voice? I thought I might
presume I did without debate or copyright.

You buy silence with tennis lessons, not sanity.
You stride in – a whiff of gin & polished leather;
lean against my bolted widow, flick ash in my vase.
Who are you anyway? You address a creation

that has veered from your storyline.
Who am I? When we meet in the asylum garden,

the moon will have bleached my hair
back to the spilled dark gold it was
the night we lay on Montgomery gravestones
unripe with youth, two hoarders of dreams.

Freedom's

a highway at dusk: the carriage rocking
while rain starts gently, strengthening.
You feel safer undercover on the way
to beginnings fused with uncertainty.
There's moorland in this freedom;
a countryside of dead cottages spread
amongst deceptive green, like emerald
oil on canvas; a lover you haven't yet met;
a docked ship, sails unfurled.

Freedom's walking alone, your small ration
sewn in the roots of your skirts.
You smell rowan, watch a kestrel stall mid-flight
to tremble on the wind, both of you starving.
Freedom can spring from the page
a tattoo artist told me while inking
a Jean Rhys line on my skin.
He spent his year in Wandsworth reading
Dostoyevsky. It emancipated him.

Ancestors crouch beside a pit of burning peat.
Bookless, they have only tongues.
Smoke rattles their fibrotic lungs, cheekbones
press like razors to the skin's surface.
The crop's failed, failed again, but their minds
are uninhabited by blight. Here's my flame
of freedom: take it's light, hand it gently
down the halls of history
to a wick that's twitching to ignite.

Rebecca de Winter: In the Dangerous Hours

How many times I've walked out of my life
through Happy Valley's sickly breath
to where the Atlantic sways & jewelled eyes
wink on a tide curdled by secrets.

Here's my boathouse, notebooks,
driftwood smoking bluish in the grate.
The mold, the mice, the rain on slate
that patters lightly – thin, then very quick.

Not now, but soon. I screw my courage.
Anger shakes that tame self, breaks its neck.
There's power in the tongue
that's unavailable to silence.

I'm not ready to forgo that, yet.

Loss Of An Animal

If love was the currency of safety you'd be here,
just-scales overspilling in your favour.

This is your twilight, your canal, your shape
on the bridge ledge perilous,

pupils swollen with adrenaline,
waxed black moons.

You tore your cattery cell to shreds.
I found you balanced on the door frame:

scattered blankets, upturned
dish, the owner's apologies

drooping in the captive air.
You were nobody's pet, insane for freedom,

but I borrowed you: a silent pact,
& you always came home –
                            till you couldn't.

Bridget O'Donnell: Hunger

When I've done all I can
to keep you living
I can live
with my own dying.
Two years in
we lie burning by turf light
too fevered to sing.
Every sickness grasps at us.

Without strength to spin
death into yarn,
we've loss without ceremony,
passing without sacrament,
muddy mouthed, nettle-lipped,
buried where we fall.

Tearing Poppies

If love were an amulet, you'd be safest.
It would shine like light at your throat,
rose gold as the moon when it floats
weightlessly upon the Calder's surface.

I sniff your baby head, undo your tears
with my sleeve on the steps of Corn Street,
framing your face with my palms.
Remember the spray of poppies

you crawled to uproot from their row-sewn
beds that morning on the Leys? Red silk
dampening my lap, you said *naughty, bad!*
jabbing your muddied dungarees.

I laughed & you slackened your grip on the oak,
tripwalking into my arms.

Vivienne Eliot: Dear Tom

At close of play I wonder why you chose me.
An object of disgust from the offset, obviously.
How could you find a greater contrast?
Perhaps that was my purpose.

In the pinch of your austerity I was grandiose.
Coupled with your cautious tongue, too loud.
I lusted, you were stone cold but once –
& *that* was not to be discussed!

I read your mother's words.
Whatever the cause, did she think it sport
that I lay prostrate & starving,
curtains pulled – your whole world
living, writing, laughing
on the lawns at Garsington?

Seven Year Itch

We sat together on a silent island.
Your voice was like a rainy afternoon in Macclesfield.
You effaced me so subtly I only realised

when CCTV ceased capturing my image.
You hated me in jeans.
I wish I could not remember your hands.

When you rated your mother
the most physically attractive woman ever,
why weren't warning sirens blaring?

The whole sprinkler system should've gone off!
I caught your suffering like a virus
mutating with my own grief, passing back & forth.

Illness became an affectation,
a way of affirming yourself,
a wardrobe even: the perpetual funereal suit.

Powdering your face like T.S Eliot,
you played with binary codes
as we folded like waves, our tide
                      going out, going out –

Dartmoor Ponies

In main-beam, drops are fireflies drawn to light,
extinguished by wipers.
Our rented grate ignites on the second match.
As the blaze flickers, I explain how my gran,
illiterate, foretold the future in flames' arrowheads.
We ignore dawn knocking,
watch moor ponies flock to thaw beneath boiler vents:
soot-maned russet, ditch-white mare,
a pregnant piebald.

In this pause, your face loses its edge
as brandy overcomes your pain.
This isn't the doorstep to happiness
but its essence, the gaping whole of it –
rain licking thin-paned glass & no alarm set.

Anosmia

After scoured lungs expel the virus,
anosmia persists. I walk the stables sniffing,
sniffing air for the essence of horses.

Nothing. Nothing rising from the banks of beech
mulch stacked where the terrier rolls
specifically in scent.

I bend to press my face into his greasy coat,
reach to pinch the rowan,
coveting an olfactory reaction.

At home, the tin of tuna
is blank air.
My nose has closed to the world.

After days in a depleted dark,
there's a slight stir in the nostrils,
or is it the throat? Woodsmoke.

I breathe to my lung-roots,
stride back to the farm in the valley's vault,
pause, allow the whiff to strengthen.

Then it comes: distinctive, blading
through blankness, a living thing.
Senses alight, I catch

a barn owl's eye effulgent in the oak;
hear as though with echolocation
bats skim mayfly from the Calder's skin.

Storm Francis

When we woke at 04.59,
scented candles were still burning,
the room pithy with orange & lemon

& a rare, monastic calm,
then peace tolling 5am.
Outside some alphabetised storm

was beating the fence thuggishly,
the stick of its force loosening planks.
You lit a spliff; I poured my Co-op wine,

mulled by the radiator's warmth.
Loosed recycling scampered the yard
like plastic vermin.

Second Time Around

Look at the copper beech, radiant
in our year of discontent, without regard
for comings and goings,
masks & skittering distance.

We must keep ourselves to ourselves,
avoid the quicksand of the season.
Surely this is the only way –
Surely this is the only way

to return to what we wanted,
what we thought we wanted.
We're curtains caught in the widow's hinge,
half-in, half-out.

At night they traipse the tow path:
hoards escaping, lugging cases
like horses tugging barges, mute
rebellion twitching in their flanks.

Night Terrors

It scares me when you whisper in your sleep;
when the dog clamps his jaw in dream,
biting down on a remembered rat, practising.

Tonight you mumble of red men.
I poke you to stir you, flick on the landing light.
You shift position, begin again: *the red men, the red men.*

When I felt pressure on my throat the exact
moment the mirror fell, I screamed myself awake:
I did it! I did that! You lifted jags of plate glass,

yawning: *a train shook it loose.*
But I lay cold as the fingertips of dawn,
wondering what spirits I'd induced,

what dark I'd drawn from to bracelet
your arm with a garland of bruises,
their purple petals already yellowing.

1 Paradise Street

Mostly I stare at the walls, pregnant,
occasionally pressing buttons on the air lock.

Assessing each resident's intoxicated state,
I let them all in regardless.

Frost sparkles on binbags of belongings
left out for evictees.

Then I'm pulling needles
from mattresses in the only pair of gloves

the hostel has: too large, they swamp
my fingers, leaving movements imprecise.

I scour arterial spray from a ceiling,
rummage cisterns finding spirits,

porn mags, foil & powder bags.
Death's so frequent here we mark a chart

(twice in 24 hours) named Seen Alive.
This shift there are two blanks.

*

In this 52 bed faux-hotel, I can't see more
than three meters ahead; corridors stutter

into sight as motion sensors activate,
their tube-bulbs flickering low light.

I knock & knock again. *Caroline?* –
this the woman who thought my altered shape

was *chocolate or drink*, too addiction-snatched
to notice the swell of a child.

We laughed together in the foyer.
She brought me stolen daffodils.

Now my ear sifts her silence.
Only my heartbeat replies.

Where Your Voice Is

When you confessed you needed silence,
I guessed your great hunger
for nothing was beginning –
that deadliest of cravings.

The doctor had reined in his tongue,
withholding a final prognosis
till you were beyond comprehension.
It wasn't compassion but cowardice.

I knew you knew. Too set on reducing
distress to flinch from tubes, drains,
the fear of roles reversing with touch.
I thought this must be love's definition:

to haul aside your terrified self.
What's more important
than the first & the final heartbeat?
As I watched the mountains of your pulse

flatten, I pictured an owl hunting
low over moorland at dusk,
the stillness of the reservoir's blue glass.
That is where your voice is.

Test Results

You're writing for your life,
there's no mistaking it.

Your fingers move in window-light,
ears closed to all but music.

Coffee heat evaporates,
a shaft of sun bisects the page,

the Biro quivers in your fingers.
Everything you strived to say

is translating itself.
Previous verse untrained lightening.

Illness has earthed you,
conducting your tongue.

Rebecca de Winter: After Diagnosis

I return with news for nobody's ears.
No shock, no tears, but loneliness mirrored by sea –
that vast expanse the weight of mercy.

How many cast themselves to the tide at first sight?
I did: born actress flailing in brine.
My mother hauled me out onto the stage.

I reject this paying & paying for ancient sins:
the guilt gene handed down, a tarnished ring.
The beech that shaded Manderley

is burning like a heart spilling its shadows.
I have my father's hair, its dark cascade,
his gift to see round corners.

I'll stomach this prognosis shot by shot.
The wild horse, whipped & groomed,
is still a wild horse.

Laura Palmer: Diary Redacted

First I navigate my ▮▮▮ self by light. ▮▮▮
▮▮▮ now I grope about in darkness, ▮▮▮
▮▮▮ parting curtains ▮▮▮ on my
own laughing image –

I leave you smoking ▮▮▮
▮▮▮ er out of it on the stairs. She
couldn't wake if the house was on fire.

Danger stiffens down the track ▮▮▮
▮▮▮ he's pre-empted me again.

Dirty sheets hood carriage windows. ▮▮▮
▮▮▮ I've not had half a gram of sleep: high &
hypervigilant –

What's this dream but clues to my own conclusion – I see
▮▮▮, it beautiful & bluish tinged

▮▮▮ Sometimes I GIVE OUT when I need
most, when I long to be held I'm gripped and bruised
▮▮▮

Help me write the verses that outlast him ▮▮▮
▮▮▮ tonight I'll plummet several rungs from the angels –

Surfacing

Lie low in the wine fumed room
listing all that unstitched you:
addictions, deceptions, loss before amends.

This is no way to navigate your morning,
no way to heal yourself.
Burn them,

these fuming regrets.
Spit on them
as London shuffles to the surface.

Stamp them into cinders
till nothing makes sense
but the music rammed in your ears.

There's no fault in how it was –
even the swiftest fish
are hooked by circumstance.

Almost free,
stream up towards that
surface gasp of light.

Shrine

In Dungloe, the Virgin's packing up her grotto,
weary of confessions.
On her shelf of rocky gorse, she's all wept out.

Trickles of water,
already unholy, intent on eroding the rock,
are withholding communions.

This is the hour of culpability,
not absolution.
Mother, the glass is dark.

Dewsbury Country Park

Today I saw a shadow on a walk
along sodden paths: a mess of thawed/
refrozen earth & rubbish rooted
in the Spen's bank, its culverts
loamy with a greasy grey.

It was a silhouette in the gloaming:
curved beak, red & white barred belly –
I stopped, watching it watch.
One wing flap flung the songbirds
from their resting places.

Methane shimmered from a vent:
those plastic tons beneath my feet
robust as on the day of manufacture.
I imagined a gull's beak sticky with garlic dip,
pigeons pecking zestfully at nappies.

This grafted park will struggle to shift purpose,
as graveyards never quite relinquish
their spirits to the housing complex.
Among bullrushes a tampon
like a bloated mouse has broken surface.

Barn Sparrows of Chernobyl

They didn't survive for long
with these mutations: females tufting
on their naturally bald brood patch;
the male's albinism a snowy bib,
his rusty breast stolen.

Nature would not accept this shift
in phenotypic traits; all was wrong,
as though a dress code had been breached.
As radiation breathed into the species,
body weights fell, along with egg clutches.

It was you who told me of that study.
The mystical part of your heart
so sure of the hour & minute its clock would stop,
you saw a finger on the shutdown switch –
sparrow-thin, nail bitten back to skin: your own.

Prank Caller

Listen,
is it ringing? Will she respond
to disturbed air in the receiver,
an exhale, a swallow, a blink?

>   Why might she insist
>   on picking up, do you think,
>   at the signal of her own distress?
>   Ask the class for a show of hands.

Explain the gap
between the crack of a broken
limb & pain grasping synapses –
pre-impact, post-impact.

>   In her first month of sobriety
>   she read 28 novels: February –
>   one per night, hoping
>   this challenge equalled silence,

hoping this was the answer
the caller required.
But the answer
was elsewhere, or the caller

>   required more than abstinence.
>   Is there someone
>   in the garden, a twitch
>   by the blackthorn?

When her sister texts
it's not quite
her sister: she suspects
an *altering of phrasing*.

        She's on the trembling lip
        of breakdown.
        Listen for the phone.
        Is it ringing?

Prayer

A prayer from one who doesn't believe in prayers
to one who doesn't believe in prayers,
this will have to travel continents
from a mill town to a sunshine state –
though that is not the weather of your heart.

We're both conscious of the ladder's movement.
Born balancing, we tolerate
intrusions we exchange for time.
I close my lids as cannulas slide in.

You stare directly at the screen
like Keats inspecting the pillow for the speck
that confirms, in arterial red,
what he already knows.

By your bravery I measure my endurance.

Coda

You sweep through the Covered Market, trench-coat flapping.
I shout out, my silent sleep-screams waking no one.

I'm jostled along, child-steps wearying.
The iron-grill is ready to come down.

Here I hang back dog-like in an underworld
of butchers & fruit stalls, watching you recede.

Where late-light promises alternative endings,
you turn onto Turl Street,

determination in your walk. It's Saturday, it's loud.
Football scores reel from bookies screens

& the whole world's ripe for your picking.
You're absorbed by the Oxford crowd.

Limerick

I had forgotten the music of silence before we arrived:
deafened by Radio 6 on high volume from 7am,

then phone calls at work – the discord of sobs
that don't quite quieten after the handset's replaced.

Diminished noise was an intake of breath.
I waited for din to recommence: the pulse of cars,

a burst of Dewsbury fireworks signalling
drugs are in – that dissonance.

I am dying for another way of being.
Through a toothless roof, a cloud of pigeons

rise, songless as smoke.
The Shannon flexes post-rain in her estuary:

a broad grey muscle, muted now,
but tuning herself to be sea.

Call Sixteen

Her adult children's Christmas presents
wrapped in May, a note in each
explaining her decision,

she couldn't say why she pulled in
when the GP number leapt onto the screen,
already set on action, thinking done,

her voice like brittle ice across a pond.
When defensiveness lapsed to disclosure,
the sobbing had a raw, drowned sound.

I kept my hand on the receiver,
slipping words along the line
like a game of Buzz Wire

where the stakes are so much higher
than start again. Despite her hatred
for each grinding hour,

she swore she'd wait for the pall to rise
if I can, she said. *If I can*.
Sixteen calls completed, fourteen to come,

I sit stiff-backed, rubbing my ruptured
disc with my free palm
till my heavy head slumps down onto my arm.

Female Tawny Waiting

I wait with her, porch shadows as my shelter.
His soothing vowels hoot at muffled distance.
From distance they disperse to absence.

Her high pitched plea increases
to insistent screeching.
I hear her listening, her dependence,

her uncertainty increasing
with the hole in his response
until anxiety becomes her sub-song.

I understand her thinking: *what if he does not come?*
The cypress hollowing, as though lightening's
struck out its centre.

If I owl to you across the wood
will you still answer?

Playing Dead

When hope's a loose leaf pressed
between two dark pages,

pick a gravestone, lie down.
Feel cold's conduction

rise from hollowed bones
into your marrowed, living bones.

Stay, unflinching.
Watch winter sun shrouding,

unveiling, shrouding.
Think of the drink

with your name on it, waiting;
your book stalled

on the crux of revelation.
Dawn will crown despite your void,

its downpour pressing
you under languageless soil.

Nothing but your words do you justice.
They are your loss-defence.

Don't leave me to imagine them.

Indigo Dreams Publishing Ltd
24, Forest Houses
Cookworthy Moor
Halwill
Beaworthy
Devon
EX21 5UU
www.indigodreamspublishing.com